Published by The Trumpet Club
666 Fifth Avenue, New York, New York 10103

ISBN 0-440-84707-9

This edition published by arrangement
with DLM Teaching Resources

Printed in the United States of America
October 1992

10 9 8 7 6 5 4 3 2 1
UPR

Old Old Witch

an old Song

Illustrated by Robert J. Lee

Editor: Tracy Moncure

Designer: Seda Sookias Maurer

A TRUMPET CLUB SPECIAL EDITION

Old Old Witch,

believe me
if you can,

Jumped on
a
broomstick

and ran!
ran!
ran!

Ran

willy
nilly

With her Toes in The air

Corn silks flying from

The old witch's hair!

Swish!

Went the broomstick!

meow!

Went the cat!

plop!

went the
hop-Toad

Sitting on her hat!

Whee! Chuckled I,

What fun!
What fun!

Halloween night

When The

Witches run!